I0843476

VALENTINES DAY

COLORING BOOKS FOR KIDS

by The Coloring Book Art Design Studio

VALENTINES DAY
COLORING BOOKS FOR KIDS

Copyright © 2019 by The Coloring Book Art Design Studio

All rights reserved. No part of this publication may be reproduced, distributed, or transmitted in any form or by any means, including photocopying, recording, or other electronic or mechanical methods, without the prior written permission of the publisher, except in the case of brief quotations embodied in critical reviews and certain other noncommercial uses permitted by copyright law.

THIS BOOK
BELONGS TO

____

____

LET'S TEST YOUR COLOR

Valentine's Day

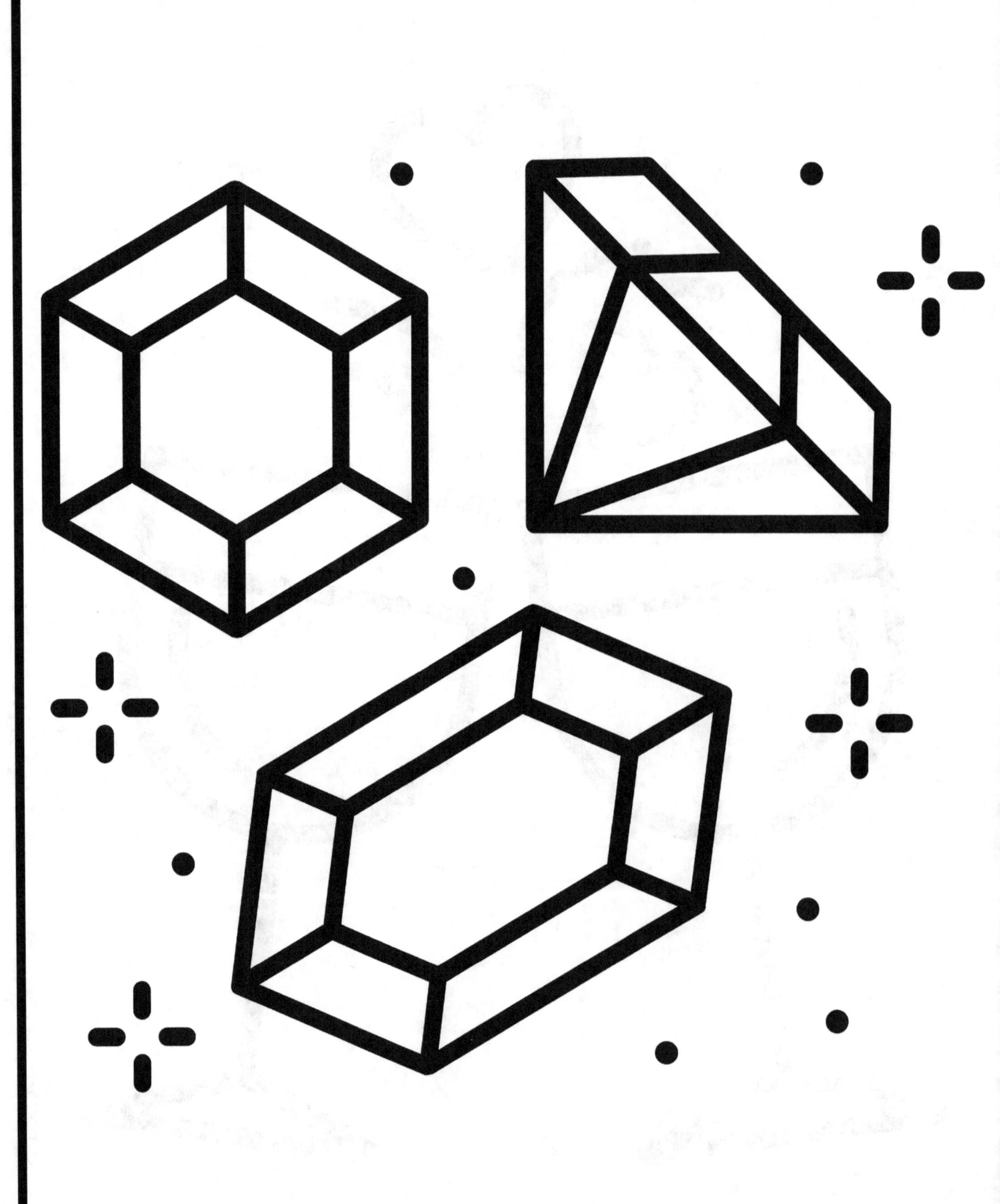

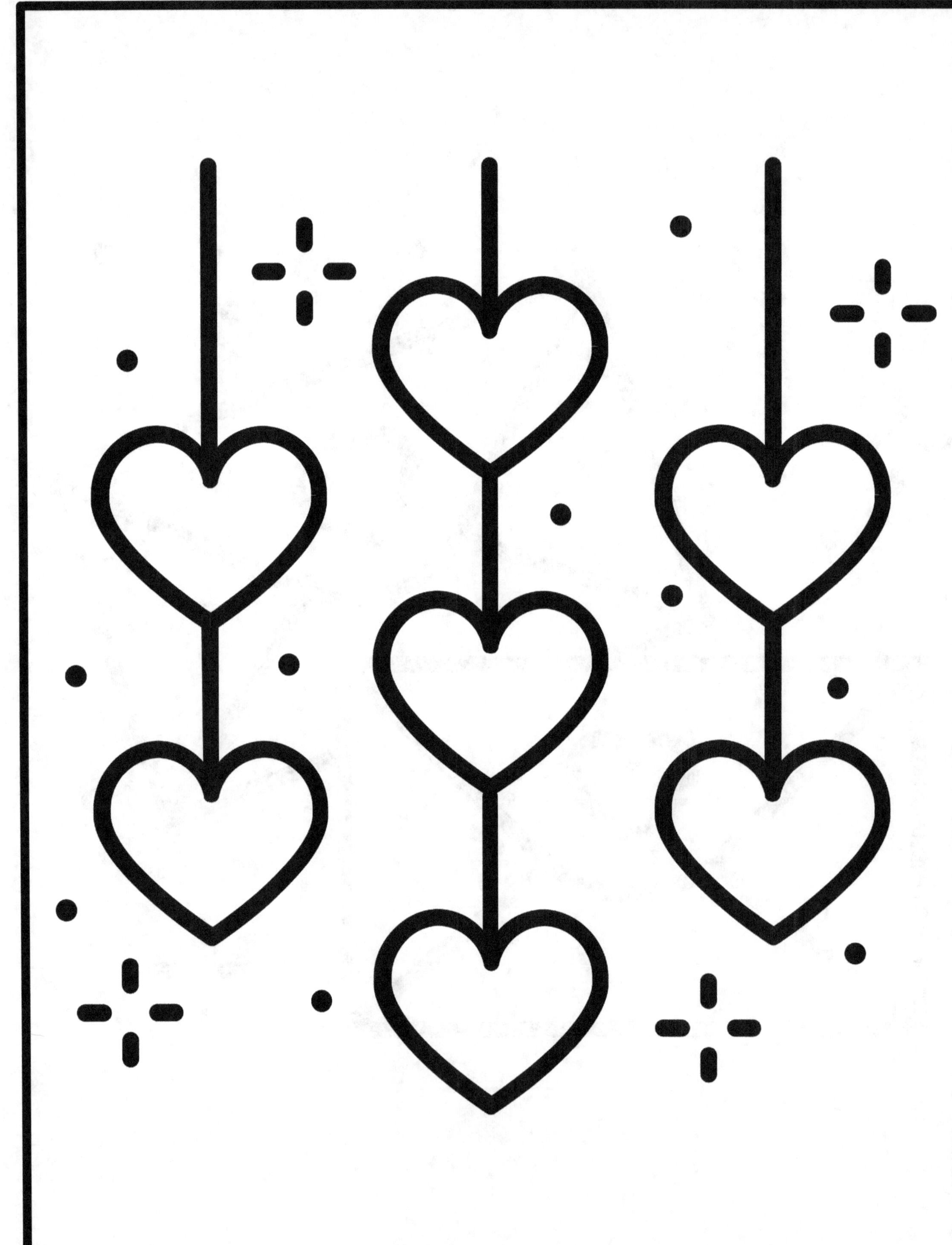

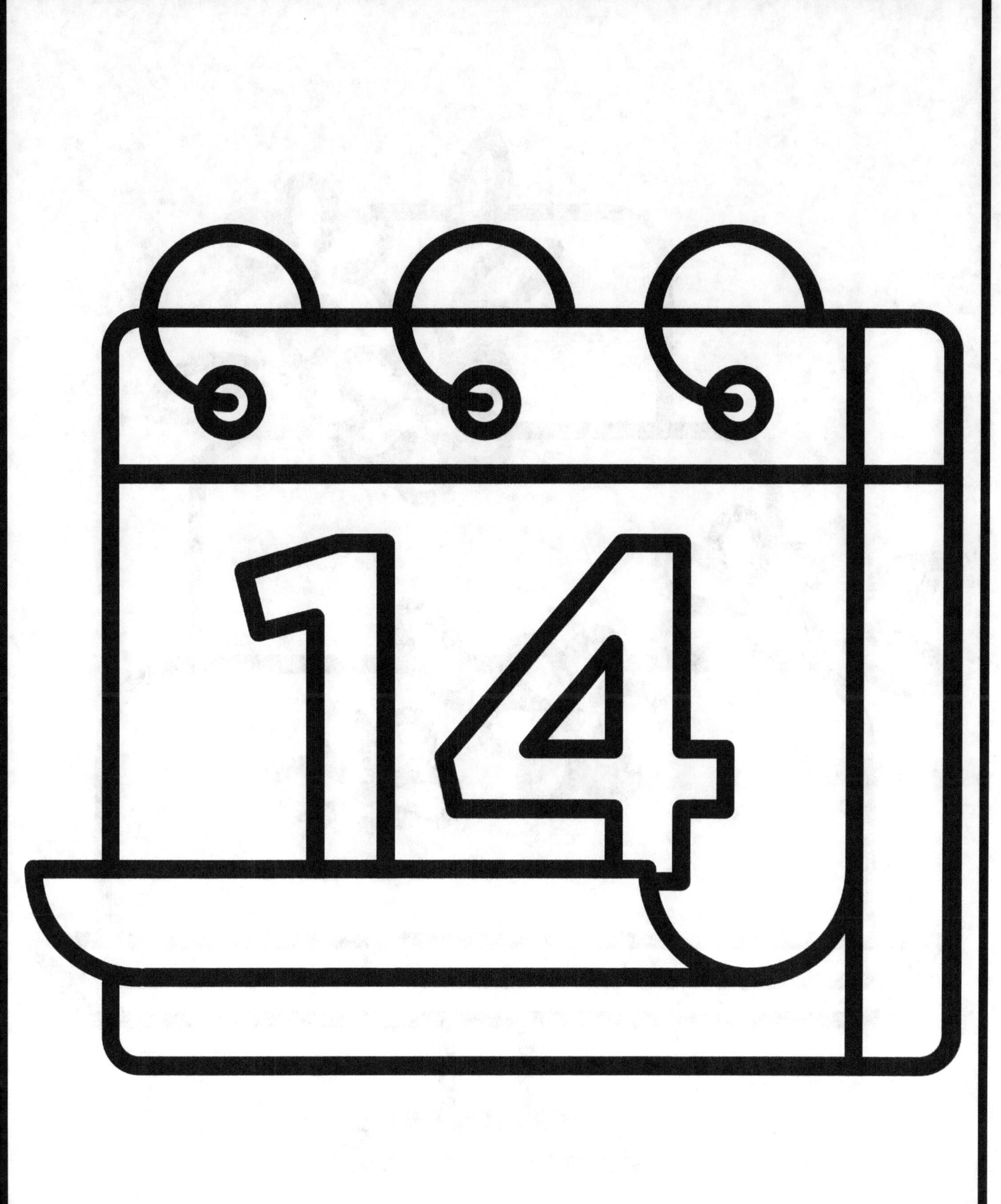

XO

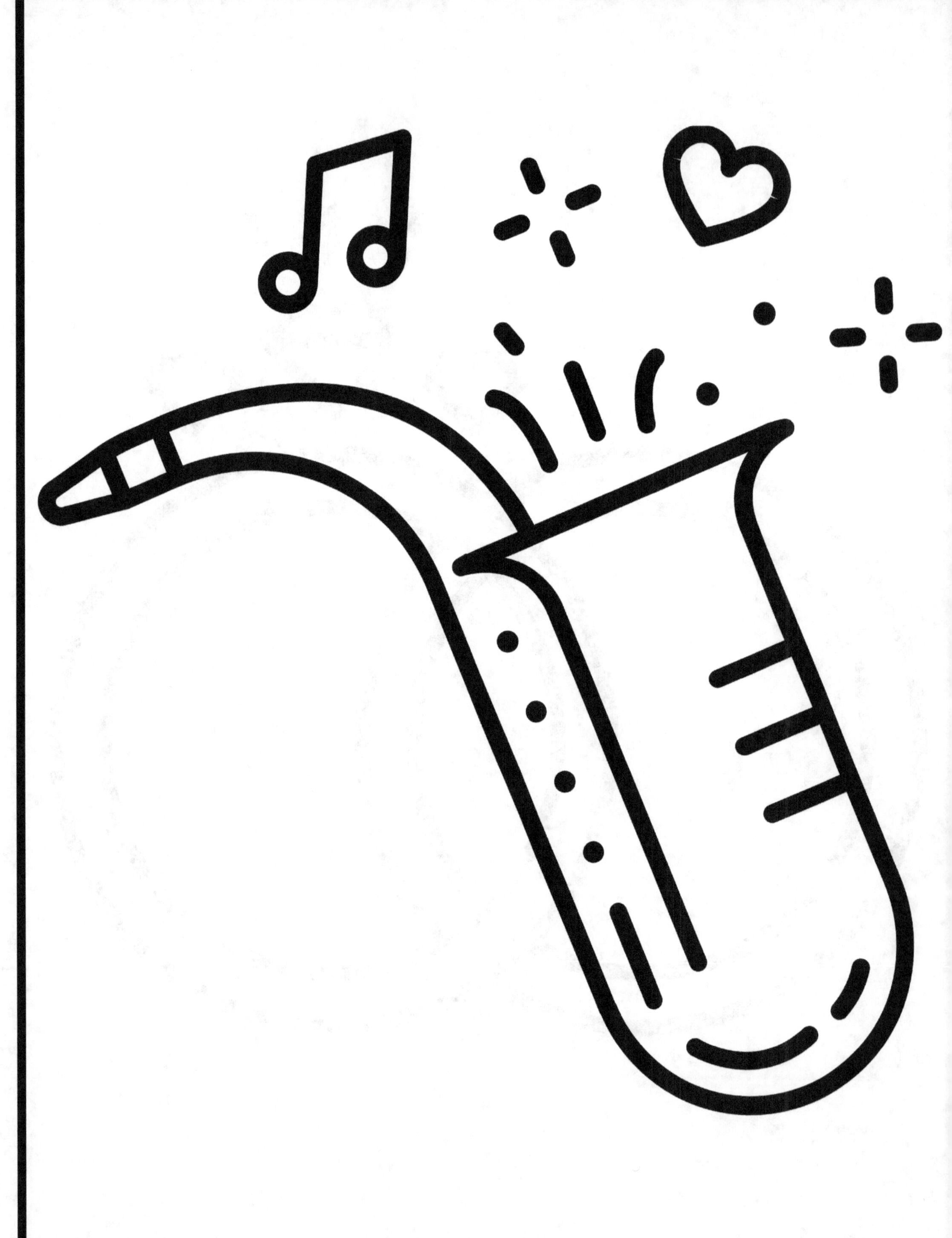

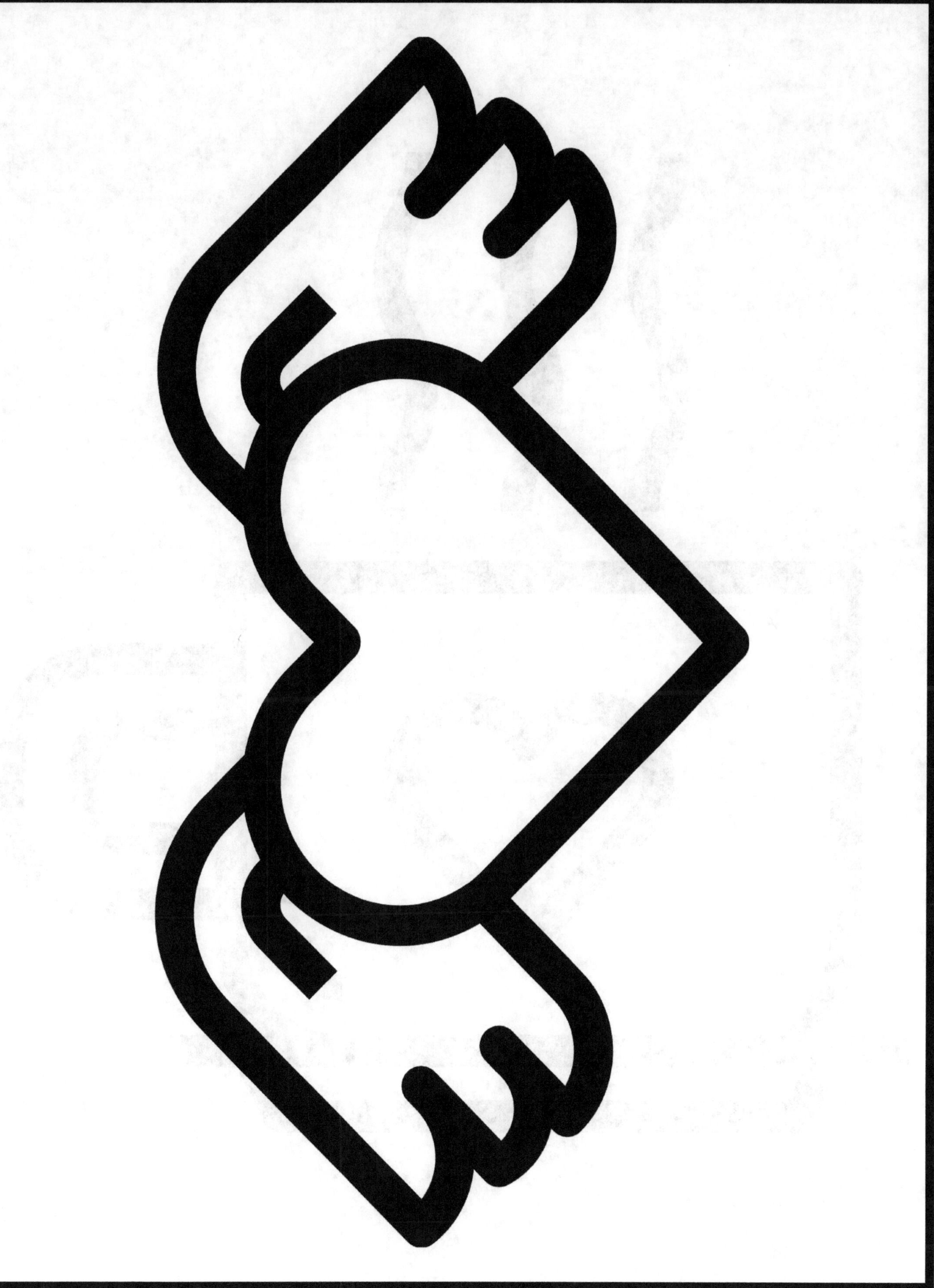

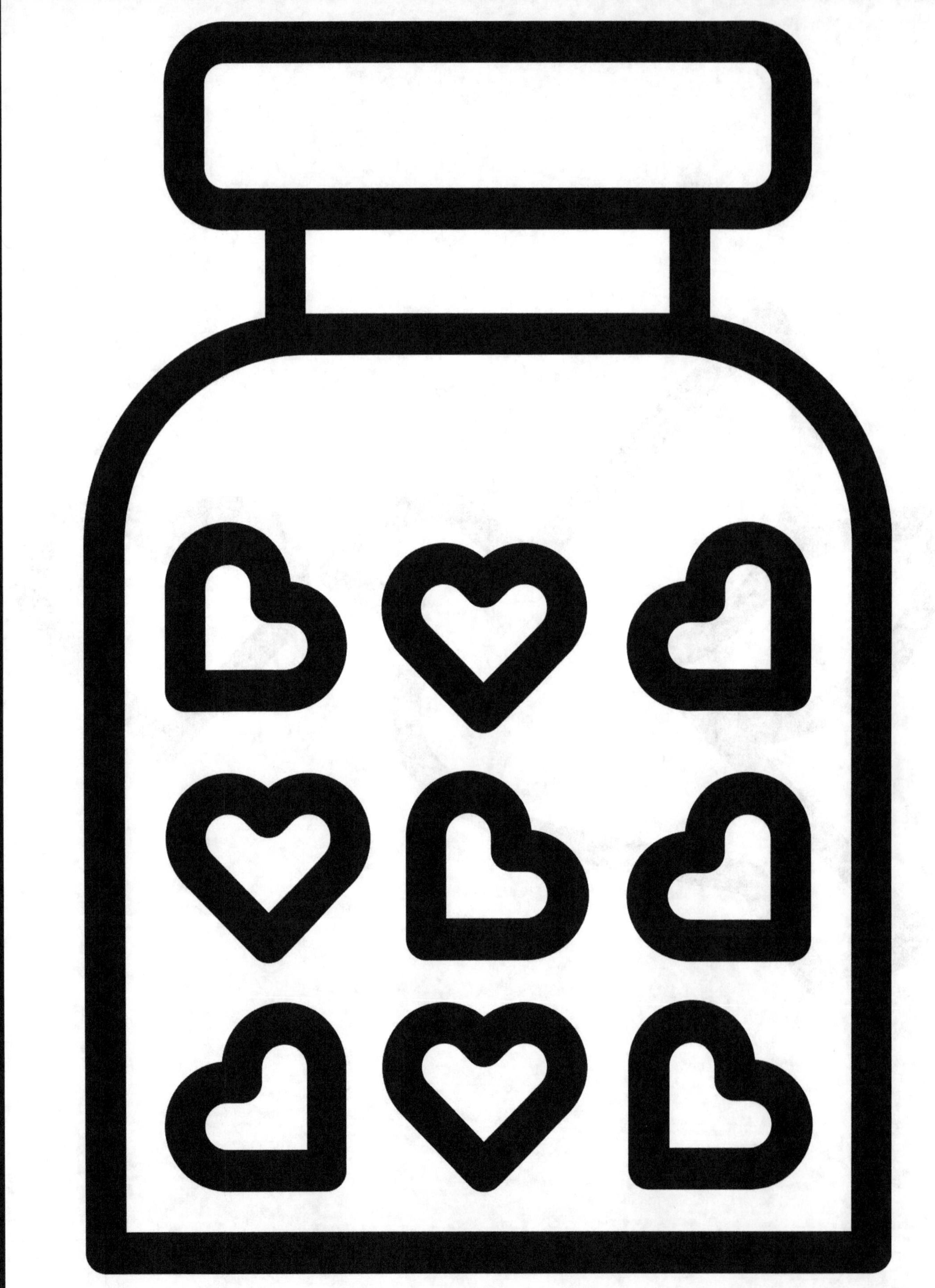

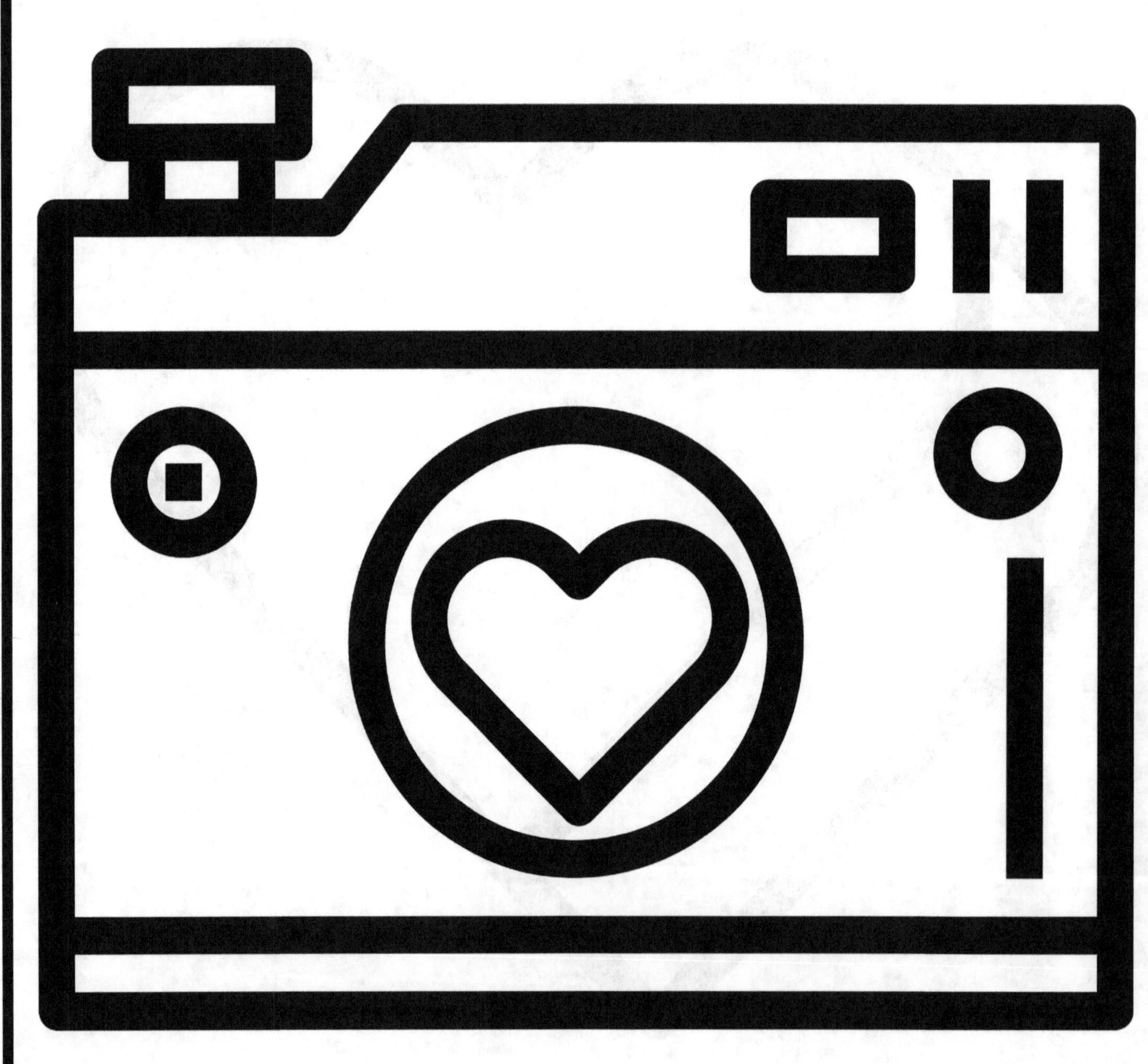

HAPPY,
Valentine's
DAY

www.ingramcontent.com/pod-product-compliance
Lightning Source LLC
Chambersburg PA
CBHW081627250726

48657CB00009B/2767